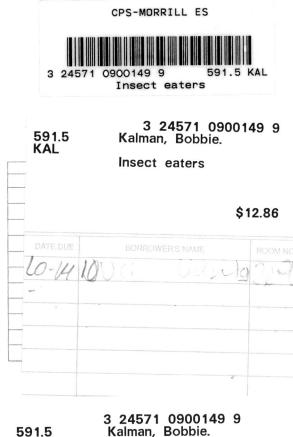

591.5
KAL

3 24571 0900149 9
Kalman, Bobbie.

Insect eaters

$12.86

DATE DUE	BORROWER'S NAME	ROOM NO.
6-14		

591.5
KAL

3 24571 0900149 9
Kalman, Bobbie.

Insect eaters

Big

Science Ideas

Insect Eaters

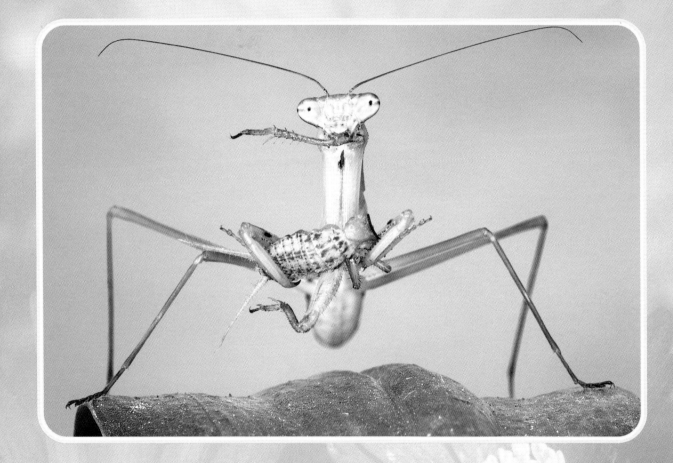

Bobbie Kalman

Crabtree Publishing Company

www.crabtreebooks.com

Big Science Ideas

Created by Bobbie Kalman

Dedicated by Katherine Kantor
To Madison and Carter Girotti — the pretty princess and handsome prince that brightened our special day with all your endless love and laughter.

Author and Editor-in-Chief
Bobbie Kalman

Research
Robin Johnson

Editor
Kathy Middleton

Photo research
Bobbie Kalman
Crystal Sikkens

Design
Bobbie Kalman
Katherine Kantor
Samantha Crabtree (cover)

Production coordinator
Katherine Kantor

Prepress technician
Margaret Amy Salter

Illustrations
Barbara Bedell: pages 4 (lizard), 10, 20 (anteater's tongue)
Jeannette McNaughton-Julich: page 20 (termite mound)
Katherine Kantor: pages 5, 14, 20 (termites), 29
Bonna Rouse: pages 4 (bat, frog, and chimp), 16, 19, 26, 27, 28
Margaret Amy Salter: pages 4 (butterfly), 8
Tiffany Wybouw: page 4 (spider)

Photographs
© Merlin D. Tuttle, Bat Conservation International, www.batcon.org: page 18
© BigStockPhoto.com: page 29 (middle)
© Dreamstime.com: title page (inset), 12 (bottom), 15 (bottom), 19, 21 (bottom), 26, 30 (top)
© iStockphoto.com: pages 10 (bottom), 12 (top), 27
© Shutterstock.com: front and back cover, title page (background), pages 3, 5, 6, 7, 8, 9, 10 (top), 11, 13 (except top right), 14, 15 (top), 16, 20, 21 (top), 22, 24, 27, 28, 29 (top and bottom), 30 (bottom left and right), 31
Other images by Adobe Image Library, Digital Stock, and Digital Vision

Library and Archives Canada Cataloguing in Publication

Kalman, Bobbie, 1947-
    Insect eaters / Bobbie Kalman.

(Big science ideas)
Includes index.
ISBN 978-0-7787-3278-5 (bound).--ISBN 978-0-7787-3298-3 (pbk.)

    1. Animals--Food--Juvenile literature. 2. Insectivores (Mammals)--Juvenile literature. 3. Insects--Juvenile literature. I. Title. II. Series: Kalman, Bobbie, 1947- . Big science ideas.

QL737.I5K34 2008   j591.5'3   C2008-905547-0

Library of Congress Cataloging-in-Publication Data

Kalman, Bobbie.
    Insect eaters / Bobbie Kalman.
        p. cm. -- (Big science ideas)
    Includes index.
    ISBN-13: 978-0-7787-3298-3 (pbk. : alk. paper)
    ISBN-10: 0-7787-3298-3 (pbk. : alk. paper)
    ISBN-13: 978-0-7787-3278-5 (reinforced library binding : alk. paper)
    ISBN-10: 0-7787-3278-9 (reinforced library binding : alk. paper)
    1. Insectivores (Mammals)--Juvenile literature. I. Title.

QL737.I5K35 2009
591.5'3--dc22   2008036592

Crabtree Publishing Company

www.crabtreebooks.com   1-800-387-7650
Copyright © **2009 CRABTREE PUBLISHING COMPANY**. All rights reserved. No part of this publication may be reproduced, stored in a retrieval system or be transmitted in any form or by any means, electronic, mechanical, photocopying, recording, or otherwise, without the prior written permission of Crabtree Publishing Company. In Canada: We acknowledge the financial support of the Government of Canada through the Book Publishing Industry Development Program (BPIDP) for our publishing activities.

Published in Canada
Crabtree Publishing
616 Welland Ave.
St. Catharines, Ontario
L2M 5V6

Published in the United States
Crabtree Publishing
PMB16A
350 Fifth Ave., Suite 3308
New York, NY 10118

Published in the United Kingdom
Crabtree Publishing
White Cross Mills
High Town, Lancaster
LA1 4XS

Published in Australia
Crabtree Publishing
386 Mt. Alexander Rd.
Ascot Vale (Melbourne)
VIC 3032

Contents

Energy from food

Living things need **energy** to stay alive. Energy is the power to move and grow. Living things get energy from the foods they eat. Some living things eat mainly plant foods. Other living things eat mainly animals. Living things that eat animals are called **carnivores**.

*This weaver bird hunts and eats **insects**. Insects are small animals.*

Insect eaters

Carnivores eat many kinds of animals. Some carnivores eat mainly insects. Carnivores that eat mainly insects are called **insectivores**. Not all insectivores are animals. Some plants also eat insects! Venus flytraps and pitcher plants eat insects.

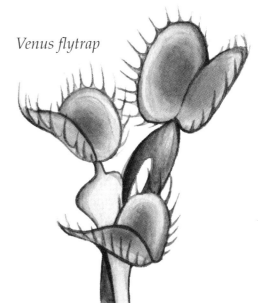

Venus flytrap

Some plants need to eat insects to stay alive. This butterfly has landed on a pitcher plant to look for food, but it may become food for the pitcher plant!

5

What are insects?

Insects are small animals with six legs. Many insects also have wings. Insects with wings can fly. Some insects do not have wings and cannot fly. There are millions of kinds of insects on Earth. This insect is a bee. It has wings.

An insect's body

An insect's body has three parts. The parts are the head, thorax, and abdomen. All insects have hard coverings called **exoskeletons**. Exoskeletons help protect the bodies of insects. Insects also have feelers called **antennae**.

Ladybugs are insects with spots.

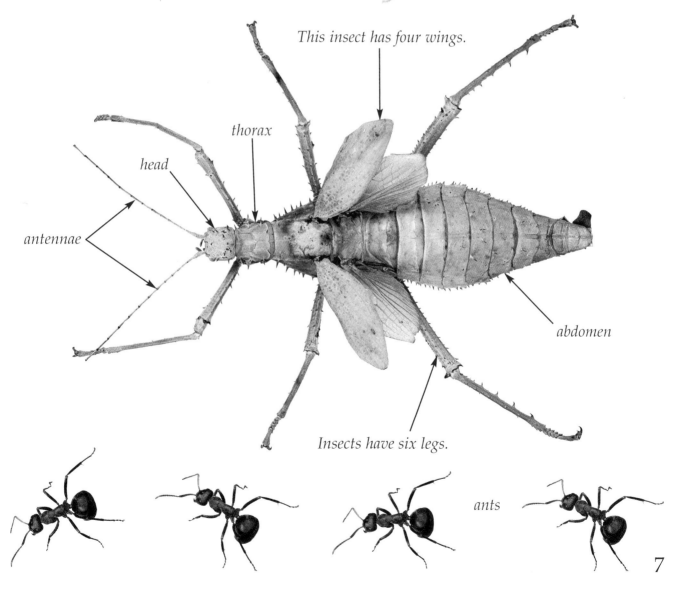

This insect has four wings.

thorax

head

antennae

abdomen

Insects have six legs.

ants

7

Spiders hunt insects

Spiders are small animals with eight legs. They are not insects, but they like to eat insects! Spiders eat flies, moths, and other **prey**. Prey are animals that **predators** hunt. This jumping spider is a predator. The fly is its prey.

Stuck in a sticky web

Many spiders spin webs made of **silk**. The webs are strong and sticky. A spider can catch many kinds of insects in its web. It bites the prey it catches and pumps **venom** into the prey's body. The venom is a poison that kills the insect.

This spider has caught a grasshopper in its sticky web. It will soon eat this insect.

9

Frogs are predators

Frogs eat flies, mosquitoes, crickets, and other insects. This frog is eating a dragonfly.

Frogs are predators, too, but they do not chase their prey. A frog stays very still and waits for an insect to come close enough to catch. The frog then flicks out its long, sticky tongue. The insect sticks to the frog's tongue. The frog pulls the insect quickly into its mouth. It swallows the insect whole.

This frog has a bee on its head. The frog will quickly catch the bee with its sticky tongue.

Frogs in trees

Some frogs live in trees. They are called tree frogs. Tree frogs have sticky toes. They use their sticky toes to hold on to branches and to climb trees. They catch the insects in the trees with their tongues.

Lunch for lizards

chameleon

Lizards are **reptiles**. Reptiles are animals with scaly skin. Snakes, alligators, and lizards are reptiles. Most lizards are insectivores. They eat crickets, grasshoppers, and other insects. The green anole lizard above is eating a cricket. This chameleon is eating a grasshopper.

Chameleon quiz

Chameleons are lizards that can change color. Why do they change color? Answer the questions below each picture to see how much you really know about chameleons!

Do chameleons change color to blend in with their surroundings so they can catch insects?

This chameleon has a fly stuck to its tongue. Name another insectivore with a sticky tongue.

Answers:

1. The colors of a chameleon do blend in, but they change mainly to show a chameleon's mood.
2. Frogs also have sticky tongues.
3. Chameleons cannot fly, no matter how many butterflies they eat!

If chameleons eat a lot of butterflies, can they grow wings and fly?

Something fishy

Fish live in water. Some insects also live in water. Mosquitoes, dragonflies, and mayflies begin their lives in ponds or lakes. The **larvae** of these insects grow in water. Larvae are young insects. Fish eat the insect larvae that they find in the water.

Dragonflies lay their eggs in water. Their larvae grow in the water until they become adults. Fish eat the larvae.

dragonfly larva

Food above the water

To find insects, fish swim near the **surface**, or top, of the water. They look for insects that have been carried into the water by wind or rain. Some insects, such as pond skaters, can walk on water. Fish can see these insects and grab them from below.

pond skater

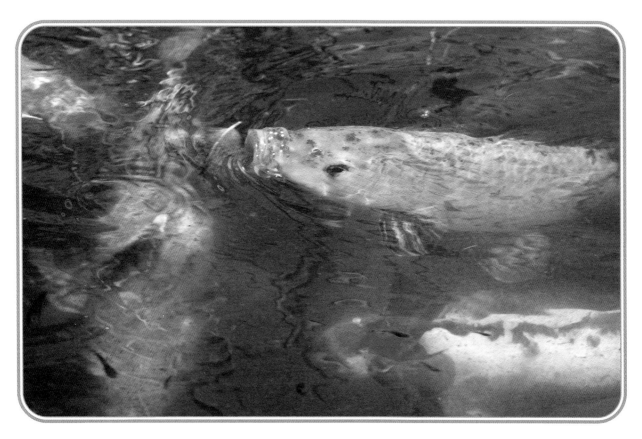

Fish catch insects that fly just above the water. They also eat insects that fall into the water.

Bird insectivores

This bird is a bee eater.

Many birds are insectivores. They fly around looking for insects to eat. Most birds use their sharp beaks to catch, hold, and carry their prey. The bird above is holding an insect in its beak. It will feed the insect to its hungry **chicks**, or baby birds.

Tap, tap, tap!

Many insects live inside trees. Woodpeckers tap their beaks on tree trunks to find insects to eat. When they hear insects inside, they use their beaks to make holes in the trees. Woodpeckers then pull out the insects with their long tongues.

Hunting at night

Bats have wings and can fly, but they are not birds. They are **mammals**. Mammals have hair or fur on their bodies. Bats are the only mammals that can fly. Most bats eat insects. They eat mosquitoes, moths, beetles, and other insects. This bat is eating a grasshopper.

Follow the echo!

Insect-eating bats hunt at night. They fly around to look for prey in the dark. As bats fly, they make high-pitched sounds. The sounds bounce back to the bats as **echoes**. The echoes tell bats about the world around them. Using echoes to find objects is called **echolocation**.

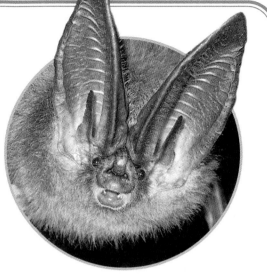

Insect-eating bats have excellent hearing. They use their big ears to hear tiny insects moving in the dark.

This bat is using echolocation to hunt. The echoes tell the bat that a moth is nearby.

Anteaters and echidnas

termite mound

Anteaters are mammals. They do not just eat ants! What other kinds of insects do they eat? Anteaters also eat termites and bees. They rip open termite **mounds** and dig up insect nests with their sharp, curved claws. They use their long, sticky tongues to grab the insects.

an anteater's tongue catching ants

*Most anteaters have long **snouts**, or noses. They use their strong sense of smell to find insects.*

Echidnas are monotremes

Echidnas are called "spiny anteaters" because they have **spines** on their bodies. They also use their noses to find insects, but echidnas are not anteaters. Anteaters are mammals that are **born**. Echidnas are **monotremes**. Monotremes are mammals that hatch from eggs.

spines ➞

Echidnas use their noses to dig up insects. They use their strong claws to tear open insect nests.

21

Insect insectivores

Some insects eat other insects. Dragonflies, robber flies, ladybugs, hornets, and praying mantises eat other insects. Some insects **ambush** their prey. To ambush is to hide or stay very still and then attack quickly. Other insects catch their prey in the air. The robber fly above has caught a moth. It pumps venom into the moth, just as a spider would.

Praying or preying?

While a praying mantis is **preying** on an insect, it looks like it is praying! It holds its front legs together to catch flies, crickets, bees, or butterflies. The insect's strong legs have sharp spines for hanging on to prey.

A praying mantis often bites off the head of its prey. Without its head, the prey cannot escape!

spines

Food for omnivores

Omnivores are animals that eat both plants and other animals. Skunks, raccoons, squirrels, mice, and most bears are omnivores. Many omnivores eat insects, as well as fruits, leaves, and other plant parts. The skunk on the left is looking for **grubs**. Grubs are insect larvae.

grub

Mice are little omnivores with big appetites! They eat insects, worms, and plant foods.

Ant "kebobs"

Chimpanzees are omnivores that eat insects. Chimpanzees are very smart animals that can use tools to help them find food. The chimpanzees above have found an ant hill. They are using a stick to pull out the ants that live inside.

This chimpanzee is eating ants. The ants are on the stick that it pulled out from the ant hill.

Plant carnivores

pitcher plant

Most plants get **nutrients** from soil and water. Living things need nutrients to grow. Some plants live in soil that does not contain enough nutrients. These plants must eat insects to get all the nutrients they need. Pitcher plants, sundews, and Venus flytraps are plants that eat insects and other small animals. The sweet smell and bright colors of these plants bring insects to them. The plants then trap the insects that visit them.

*Sundews have a sticky liquid on their leaves. Insects think the liquid is **dew**. Dew is drops of water. These dragonflies were caught by the sundew plants when they tried to take a drink of dew.*

This Venus flytrap has trapped a fly.

Venus flytraps

Venus flytraps have leaves that are like jaws. When an insect walks or lands on a leaf, the leaf quickly snaps shut. The insect gets trapped inside. The leaf then **digests**, or breaks down, the body of the insect.

The fly is now inside the flytrap.

27

Important animals

Insectivores are very important. Without these plants and animals, there would be too many insects on Earth. Some insects are **pests**. Pests are animals that harm or bother people. Some insects sting or bite. Insects such as mosquitoes carry **diseases** that can make people sick.

Bats can eat hundreds of insects each night!

Bee-eaters are birds that eat bees and wasps. Bees and wasps sting people and animals.

Helping people

Other insects hurt people's **crops**. Crops are plants that farmers grow for food. Insectivores help people by eating these pests. Ladybugs are insects that eat aphids. Aphids are tiny pest insects that can destroy gardens and crops.

aphids

ladybugs

Giant anteaters eat thousands of ants and termites each day! Many kinds of ants are pests. Termites often cause damage to people's homes by eating the wood in the buildings.

Food for many animals

Insects are food for many kinds of animals. Insects are eaten by spiders, frogs, lizards, birds, mammals, and other insects. The dragonfly on the right is eating a smaller insect.

The bird on the left caught a dragonfly for its dinner. Later, the bird might be eaten by a screech owl. Insects and insectivores are food for many kinds of animals!

Does that bug you?

You may not know it, but you are an insectivore, too! Did you know that ground-up bugs are part of bread, cereal, and soup mixes? Insects are in your fruit, vegetables, and drinks, too. The reason you have insects in your food is that **pesticides** do not kill all the insects in crops.

It's just meat!

Insects contain the same kinds of nutrients as meat does. If you were ever lost in the woods, you could stay alive by eating grubs or crickets. In some countries, people think of insects as treats! Which insects would you like to try?

Fried cockroaches, cicadas, grasshoppers, and crickets are popular foods in China.

Glossary

Note: Some boldfaced words are defined where they appear in the book.

born Coming out live from a mother

crop Plants grown by people to be used as food

dew Tiny drops of water that form in the morning

disease A serious illness

echo A wave of sound that repeats another sound

echolocation The use of echoes to locate objects

insect A small animal with six legs and a hard covering on its body

insectivore An animal or plant that eats mainly insects

larvae Young insects that have hatched from eggs but are not yet adults

mammal A person or warm-blooded animal that has hair or fur, a backbone, and is born live; female mammals make milk in their bodies to feed their babies

mound A structure made by termites

nutrient An important part of food that helps living things stay healthy

pesticide A chemical used to kill insects

predator An animal that hunts and eats other animals

preying Hunting prey

silk A strong, thin, sticky thread that spiders make inside their bodies

spine A sharp, needle-like body part

Index

Printed in the U.S.A. - CG